Isolating One's Priorities in a Time of Crisis

poems by

Jan Harris

Finishing Line Press
Georgetown, Kentucky

Isolating One's Priorities in a Time of Crisis

Copyright © 2021 by Jan Harris
ISBN 978-1-64662-667-0 First Edition
All rights reserved under International and Pan-American Copyright Conventions.
No part of this book may be reproduced in any manner whatsoever without written permission from the publisher, except in the case of brief quotations embodied in critical articles and reviews.

ACKNOWLEDGMENTS

Many thanks to the following publications where these poems first appeared:

Yes, Poetry: "Many Worlds Theory"
The West Trade Review: "Exclusion Zone"
Portland Review: "Mass Extinction," "After the Sun Goes Out," "Chrismation"
Camas: "Marauders All"
Exposition Journal: "Walking Poem"
The Rumpus: "The Rashomon Effect"
Waxing and Waning: "Modern Homesteading" (as "St. Paul's Cathedral")
"The Paradox of Choice" (as Erasure Poem from Baedeker's Greece, "Delphi, 140)
"The Spirit of the Prophet is Subject to the Prophet" (as (Erasure Poem from *Muirhead's Blue Guide: Ireland*, "An Outline of Irish History, xi")

The poem "Time and Duration" takes its title from the work of Henri Bergson

Publisher: Leah Huete de Maines
Editor: Christen Kincaid
Cover Art: Alex Anderson
Author Photo: Timothy Ross
Cover Design: Elizabeth Maines McCleavy

Order online: www.finishinglinepress.com
also available on amazon.com

Author inquiries and mail orders:
Finishing Line Press
PO Box 1626
Georgetown, Kentucky 40324
USA

Table of Contents

Mass Extinction 1

Many Worlds Theory 2

Asteroids like Rabbits 3

Chrismation 4

Episodic Memory 5

The Paradox of Choice 6

A Handbook for Resilience 7

After the Sun Goes Out 8

Eschatological Ruminations 9

Time and Duration 10

Thucydides 12

Radio Silence 13

The Average Mean 14

Isolating One's Priorities in a Time of Crisis 15

What You Don't Prepare for 17

Linear Super Position 18

Marauders All 19

Cognitive Flexibility 20

Season's Greeting 21

Latter Day Saints 22

Home Storage 23

Post-Apocalyptic DSMV 24

Exclusion Zone 25

Modern Homesteading 26

just a stranger in a strange strange place —Kevin Morby

*for Martone my teacher
and
for my students
il miglior fabbro*

Mass Extinction

we cannot know what evolutionary biologists will call this age   we cannot know which of our offspring   will survive at night we count them and wonder   which one will it be we search their sleeping faces for resistance   we are looking for a future we will build   with what we have left   we understand that geological memory drives vertebrates   we know that once we waited a million years   to crawl towards water's edge   we have learned that observations   produce evidence   and in each mass extinction the emphasis   is on the quick not the dead   we observe long vacant cities   teeming with rats and pigeons dark seas replete with giant jellyfish   we do not live in an elegant age   we're unable to reproduce the cultured aesthetic of sheep in a ha-ha   aquatic swans   or the tenuous expansion of coral reefs   ours is an age of salination   desiccation   interminable heat   we muster our resources unsure of our end   our final ablation an offering   for the black holes who hold our universe together

Many Worlds Theory

There is a reality that we perceive
Then there is the limitation of our eyes
Things are only collections of measurements and outcomes in various situations
For example two possibilities are both real in two separate universes
Especially when observed by two isolated bystanders
There may be more than two observers
There may be as many universes as there are observers
Think of these universes as strings
Each universe a string running parallel to the other strings
Parallel strings avoiding intersection and entanglement
Until one string begins to wind itself around the others
Creating a proximity but not perhaps a cohesion
We can use this theory to provide a sort of explication
Our lives ran parallel until we met in the knot of disaster
Our intertwining presented two alternatives
    A. to collapse everything and begin again
    B. to recognize the limits of universes

Asteroids like Rabbits
    (Erasure Poem from The Story of the Sun, 19)

the diligent astronomer
augmented a somewhat
tedious process with
laborious charting
   time passing disclosed
adjacent light whose
existence made known
the fertility of asteroids
   that in course
discovered a planet

Chrismation

we practice adapting   to the disintegration of locks   the pitfalls of
growing hydroponic lettuces   loose dogs in the alley   today there are
purple circles   floating in the stratosphere   we can tell they're
cylindrical   a deduction made from our knowledge   of opacity and
shade   whether the circles   are really purple   we do not know
purple is what we see   and what we have   learned about light
particles   is they bear witness   to the limits of our perception
much like our children's   refusal to believe us   when we tell them
that limes grew on trees and how succulent limes were   tree limes
and all the luscious things   belong elsewhere   they are ancient
remnants   of a forgotten anointing

Episodic Memory

when one system collapses another emerges -Xenophon

when we look at the frontier we know we can survive
deep in us the memory of arid plains and savannahs
solacing us through our hard scrabble expansion

long ago we learned how to put our feet on the soil
we bid farewell to the shelter of trees
we did not know what lay ahead of us

the deep gutturals of the Neanderthal
even the sounds of our own voices unimaginable
we only had the caprices of thunder to bring us fire

the strength of our hands to grapple with wolves
rocks to hurl at predators lurking in the water
we hold these traumas in our bones

we know our people can harvest light from the storm
we live in the memory of what we have endured
soaring words and inspiration are not necessary to us

now we follow our leaders less willingly
each one of us responsible for their own acts of virtue
like these shadowy ancients adrift miles home

we want to believe that ethics will protect us
that we strive to do the right thing in the right way
that our protocols motivate our progress towards civilization

but we know only genetic nostalgia drives us forward
it is our rootlessness that agitates our resolve
and causes us to cry out one voice at the sight of the sea

The Paradox of Choice
(Erasure Poem from Baedeker's Greece, "Delphi, 140")

the most ancient
seemed to invite
the dragon
slew five days
after its birth
brought hither
probably an error
the instigation
of pilgrims and
the destroyed

A Handbook for Resilience

we used to worry about expiration
dates blow outs work life balance
personal efficiency kettle bells safety
helmets   we would ask each other
what seem like strange questions to
us now   is my plane on time or what's
your mantra but should we trust this
Uber driver and how can we develop
better habits for productivity and
happiness   our predicament has freed
us from the oppression of quarterly
target goals bike commutes having
three children whose monograms
match on all their school accessories
   thankfully we don't have any more
conversations about finding our passion
or clutter free living   we still speak of
grit but it's the friction we feel when
our scouts spot tribes of free ranging
West Virginians armed and scaling
down our canyon's walls   we slide our
tongues across our teeth as we push
with our shoulders to close the gates
   we spit the sand and sediment out
of our mouths as we bolt them

After the Sun Goes Out

and who could have imagined this cold
there is no more joy and no time for
simple pleasures like strawberry jam and
the other ways we spent our time as we
watched the last sputtering of light fall
towards us it took seven years for those
final flashes to reach the surface and the
whole time we dreamt of a superhero
who was coming to save us every night
we would warm our bread by the fire and
lather it with strawberry jam as if to say
we are not afraid of the hypothetical dark

Eschatological Ruminations

when we're scavenging in deserted towns
we love to find apocalyptic film reels and
DVDs full of meteors alien invasions
blackholes   our favorites are the religious
movies where god or god's son or god's
prophet descends through parting clouds
to reveal patches of the bluest sky
   at one time we all believed like this that
our lives would tumble on and then when
no one was paying attention in a fanfare
god would intervene   yet despite all of our
fixations on the last days we never imagined
the whistling sounds of radio-magnetic grass
on abandoned golf courses   where we camp
because the sand bunkers have unobstructed
views of both horizons   perhaps this explains
our fascination with these movies as they try to
foreshadow what would be   each quaint fantasy
causing us to chuckle as our ancestors chuckled
at those who clung to their belief in a flat earth
   sometimes no matter how we steel ourselves
we weep when the credits are backgrounded
by pastoral landscapes if only the pristine green
fields if only the aqua sky peeling back to the
sounds of celestial trumpets   we cannot indulge
these reckless hopes of deliverance   the earth
is indeed a globe whose elliptical orbit barrels
us toward infinity   and even though it rends our
hearts to confess it no rapture is coming to save us

Time and Duration

time
we accept that time is spatial
twenty four hours equals one rotation
an incremental measure of distance
our movement through space is time
we record the heterogeneity of space and time
each unit implies some time has passed
each unit suggests motion
we can chart our progression

duration
we do not think time is discrete
our past presses on our present
we carry the flow of memory
our ancestors knew ceaseless migration
each day they walked many miles
ice caps stretched out and shrank
the sun was darkened by ash clouds
they flowed like time through temperate zones
we feel the weight of their lived experiences
our bodies the one boundary
between their time and ours

time
each day a different space
but the same boundary of time
we know the time it takes us to reach the woods
we can measure the woods' circumference
we estimate how long it will take to circumnavigate them
we avoid all blank spaces unmapped by memory
we obey each meticulous border
where time has forbidden us to go

duration
our past presses in on us
tracing its tentacles through our present
the shudder of déjà vu
we do not have tools to process new data
we predict duration walking backwards
we have perfected building models to scale
we are prepared for what we will encounter
so long as it resembles all we left behind

Thucydides
My work is not a prize work for performance

we share his motives   an impulse to decipher   what had happened we aspire to be objective not poetical to record the complexity of events austere and convoluted   not a unity   we do not invoke foundational myths it is difficult to elicit the truth of human dealings   even when we have   lived through them   it is hard to understand the decisions humans make even when we have made them ourselves we doubt the historian's theories   the causes and wars we distrust the syntax   of our tight-lipped assumptions about how cities work about how we might behave   we concentrate on things as they are and   not what they may be   we resist exoticizing and relinquish our judgements of aliens   we hold to our task   to pick at the web of human relations so future citizens might avoid extremes seasons of plague and the rhetoric of oligarchs   we would leave behind something   not a grand possession   for all time perhaps a guide for   societies for   how they fall   apart   or at least a record

Radio Silence

    we should have recognized all the whispers about zombies were either recycled urban legends or poor attempts at satire   when the worst was over after the marauding tribes settled down we started migrating back to where we had come from   we walked through shells of suburbs and condo communities whose names began to merge in our minds like summer camp photo collages   Stone Manor Velocity Steeplechase   we didn't loiter at their mangled security gates or violate their charred no soliciting signs   it was so deep our wistfulness for pool days at the clubhouse the guest sign-in clipboard half-hour rotations of sunburnt life guards   when sources of potable water were readily available we'd remember our past leisure and follow the temptation to creep up to a busted call box

    we'd gingerly press the send button as we whispered into the speaker *we've made it this far*   each of us longing for one familiar voice to shatter that implacable stillness

The Average Mean

some flirt with believing in providence but we cannot tarry in those illogical assumptions

we have only the proofs of our enduring bodies and our hearts' variables of joy and sorrow

we count our joys on our hands this day's safety or a night's sleep without rustling sounds in the shadows

our sorrows are beyond counting and lie scattered around us in the radon dust covering our planet's irradiated surface

we recognize the miscalculations of our past we were solving the wrong equations

we did not know that our joy was a rational integer our sorrows a web of congruent relations

we have had to teach ourselves a new arithmetic

Isolating One's Priorities in a Time of Crisis

    nothing in the parlor will help us survive
making it difficult to justify the bone china
let alone throwing one last tea party   please
don't be afraid that once the nuclear dust settles
we'll pine for the bygone tea parties of this world
 but quite frankly we do wonder if the next world
resounds with the clinking of saucers against cups
announcing the dawn of new gods and their half-god
half-ceramic offspring   anyway we can barely open
the parlor door due to all the throw pillows   we do
not know who leaves them there but what can we
expect when the sirens began blaring we let the
neighbors inside   so only lately we have realized
that one of them is stockpiling throw pillows in our
parlor   however if we take the evacuation orders
seriously these pillows may be a godsend when we
have to do some quick packing   now it's not
escaping the end times or the looming mushroom
cloud that really troubles us   rather it's that these
harbingers herald the end of all swans   who always
projected such placidity and swan-likeness gliding
across lakes   we do assume we will have lakes and
parlors in our new homes   homes abandoned by
those who have exchanged the last days of their worlds
for the last days of ours   we are speculating but
images of swans in new lakes consoles us makes us
forget all the throw pillows we have had to endure
   in our current living arrangements we dare not peel
the duct tape from our windows and hurl each pillow
along with our hoarding neighbors into what is left
of the yard   even though there would be some joy
for us to see the infrared light refract off our impeccably
polished sideboard   when we think about it there we
could find a reason to keep our chins up if we could
take just one swan with us   once it's safe to finally
shake off the neighbors and leave these miserable

pillows behind   we could strike out boldly steeled by
our hope that tomorrow or maybe the next day we
would discover a lake

What You Don't Prepare For

deep cold barrages us
we remember the stars
and wonder if they did
not die as the astronomers
tell us   it is perhaps wiser
to listen to iterant gurus
who wander about with oil
lamps declaring that the stars
are not dead but are hidden
from one another like us

Linear Super Position

we feel most sorry for quantum theorists no one cares anymore about wave function if electrons are particles or spread out like clouds it doesn't matter now we cannot linger on what we are or what we might be reality is what we perceive we cleave together to survive we disperse after hope has eroded we admit we could be living an existence in another branch of the multiverse secure in other lives or we remain here where the big bang's microwave radiation is only one of many radiations we fear theorists try to inspire us but we lack their imagination how do we exchange life or death for the possibilities of alive   and dead death stalks us from many angles   while life builds our shelters surrounded by razor wires our outcomes are uncertain theorists remind us physics cannot give existence purpose establishing a discriminate value is our responsibility what we see when we look at things is different than what they are we built our own box and placed ourselves inside we've been moving through life and death at equal speeds we cannot know which one the species who comes after us will encounter when they open the lid

Marauders All

in the day-glow light
our old skins cells flake
off and drape across
the zoysia grass an
offering to long-dead
microbes who spun
themselves into
complex beings
while they shivered
in a toxic sea with
no atmosphere just
that same star
enticing the reckless
protozoa who swam
towards its beacon
sailors in a maelstrom
lured by the smuggler's
lantern only to run
aground on a more
perilous shore where
we begin

Cognitive Flexibility

we don't judge the new survivalists or the post millennial cults
their conclusions seem logical in the light of current events
the end drew nigh and we were not prepared
we skipped the rapture and plunged headfirst into these tribulations
the jack-booted thugs came and they were our neighbors
we are finding our way back to fellowship but it is a perilous practice
to release our fear and allow our offspring to wonder in the garden
to watch their precious DNA drip
when they are pricked by thorns
in these moments of tender tragedy we heed the call
to gather our makeshift tribes together
and circle our squatters hut with booby traps
we too are motivated by the vectors of love and fear
we live in the Venn diagram between them
each of us entwined in their corresponding sway

Season's Greetings

we pass clement evenings foraging among the wreckage
of shop local boutiques and chain drugstores   we concede
it's sentimental to unearth fragments of Easter baskets
faded banners greeting cards that remind us   *you're going to
make it champ hang in there thinking of you sending deepest sympathy*
we no longer know what day marks our children's birthdays
we no longer have non-lunar indications for spring   now in
the warm season we can breathe easy because other subdivision
squatters are no longer trying to sabotage our ad hoc solar panels
but we still feel the need to secure our gardens with
patchy strips of piecemeal barbwire   once and a while we come
in from our labors to discover someone has left a mangled card
outside our door   and when we open it we read incongruous
messages *lordy lordy look who's forty or bon voyage, happy retirement*
but scrawled along the card's weathered edges we find more
appropriate greetings written in beet ink *happy root harvest day or
rainy days are the best days to test all your locks*   we hesitate unsure if
the card was left as a happy salutation or as the confession of guilty
party for something we may have already lost   after we check our
locks and examine the trap wells around the garden's perimeter we
take the card inside   as the day darkens we light the hurricane
lamps   to read our card again and again relishing life's uneven acts
of kindness   we appreciate our neighbors' beneficence and
generosity   each object they treat with gentleness exposes them to
new   threats as do we

Latter Day Saints

> *it is a wonderful thing to learn thoroughly how to die.*
> —Seneca

flies keep getting into the house
we open the windows to let them
escape because we think there may
be enough death   because we don't
need to accrue any more karma if
there is karma for something like
taking the life of a fly   but our flies
won't take the exit route would
rather stay in this box they have
chosen   maybe they're ascetic and
want to abandon their wanton fly lives
  each day growing more impervious
to the outdoor picnic or the magnetism
of a city dump   our flies yearn only for
the clarity of light to buzz buzz against
the unrelenting window pane   to endure
the midday purgation we reserve for
disregarded house plants   each one a
virgin mystic whose desiccated corpse
sanctifies our south facing room

Home Storage

once we called this wariness anxiety now we call it awake
to be watchful of sounds the wind brings
to know there is more lurking in the gale than the storm
we lost the security of motion sensor lights and satellite alarm systems
we foster a tenuous peace by keeping ourselves in order
we forebear our human proclivity towards confabulation
we gaze into the reservoir of who we might become
to discover new threats
years of faulty provisions we store within ourselves
poorly sealed mason jars and other efforts at magnanimity
we cannot see the mold with our eyes but
we smell it when we open the lid
we dream of verdant summers and a blight free harvest
we are hopeful that we will lay better provisions next year

Post-Apocalyptic DSMV

we saw that some of us had been separated
from themselves and their reintegration
into the whole was not a possible outcome

we could not replace their inner vacancies
we could not estimate the size of their lonesomeness
or fill them with the vanities of optimism and hope

our consolations left us feeling bereft and when
they began to wander away from us we felt relief
like we had rolled some fantastical boulder downhill

as their backs receded in the distant we rejoiced
watching their sorrowful auras lift from our settlements
leaving a rainbow-like promise above us in the sky

these departures make the neat order of our lives possible
we knew some would return to us when they were ready
we are a social species and it is our sadness which leads

us back to one another but later in our tents we thought
of others who would not come back and how in times
past we had amused ourselves by capturing lighting bugs

because they could not hide and were so easy to find
we thought of all the bugs we had trapped in jars
we misapprehended their shuddering luminescence

as they rippled through the night we caught them
thinking that they would be lights to guide us back
across the summer yard to the safety of our thresholds

we overlooked their need for well ventilated spaces
forgetful that their luminosity was more circumstantial
and fragile than our imaginations could welcome

Exclusion Zone

in these latter days we have embraced an enigmatic
vocation   we stand in abandoned cul de sacs and
radiate love   we are glad of gainful employment
all the infrastructure we had known collapsed
   we had to abandon the luxury of occupations
they are no longer available to us   we miss them
now we can only radiate love although it is hard labor
   we stand in cul de sacs point our chests towards
discarded mc-mansions and their derelict hedges   we
begin to oscillate with the intractable surge that vibrates
between our ribs   love pulsates with a ferocious
diffraction like the nuclear fallout that is still releasing
in the forests   we cannot know if our work changes
anything   in hopeful times pop songs told us love
could move mountains that no mountain could stop love
   but we admit there is no empirical evidence to support
that this was ever true   yet rumors persist that deer and
foxes have returned to Chernobyl's exclusion zone that
   wildflowers crowd its meadows and in the shadows
green things begin to grow

Modern Homesteading

> *We are being taught by clouds of star particles how to love.*
> —Duncan Trussell

stretch the map across the floor and pick a blue
dot which one we choose doesn't matter
the universe unfolds in ceaseless combinations
  we are the map we are the dot we have seen
them all been them all in 10,000 iterations   so
familiar like a motion that wakes us in the night
and we know that something is there because we
feel it breathing against us reaching past twilight's
 consciousness   its intimacy neither male or female
not self or other not same but different it pulls from
time's frontier an event horizon subsuming our
private apocalypses   it whispers that we too must
die and death will be sooner than we know yet we
will be braver than we think because the light inside
is the light outside   and it's already shining around
us as we begin to inhabit a world we had known but
waited for this moment to discover   waited to
catch our breath before plunging into that white
burning we call existence

Jan Elaine Harris (she/her) is a tenured Associate Professor of Writing at Lipscomb University in Nashville, TN. She earned her MA and PhD at The University of Alabama. Recent poems have appeared, or are forthcoming in *Yes, Poetry, The West Trade Review, HERWords, The Portland Review, The Rumpus,* and *The Exposition Journal.* She lives in East Nashville with her partner, Tim, and their two perfect GSPs, Malloy and Astrid-June.

www.ingramcontent.com/pod-product-compliance
Lightning Source LLC
LaVergne TN
LVHW041516070426
835507LV00012B/1610